Nancy Hall

Spellwell

Book

B

Educators Publishing Service, Inc.
Cambridge and Toronto

Cover design by Hugh Price

Art by Alan Price

Educators Publishing Service, Inc.
31 Smith Place, Cambridge, Massachusetts 02138

May 2001 Printing

CONTENTS

Copy the words your teacher gives you under Classroom Words. Fold this page back along the dotted line so that only the Pretest column shows. Cover page 3 so you cannot see it. Write the words your teacher dictates.

Spell*well* Words	Corrections	Pretest
1. club	_____	1. _____
2. crib	_____	2. _____
3. dragon	_____	3. _____
4. glass	_____	4. _____
5. planet	_____	5. _____
6. slips	_____	6. _____
7. spilled	_____	7. _____
8. strap	_____	8. _____
9. swims	_____	9. _____
10. trip	_____	10. _____

Outlaw Words

11. flew	_____	11. _____
12. blew	_____	12. _____
13. blue	_____	13. _____

Classroom Words

14. _____	_____	14. _____
15. _____	_____	15. _____
16. _____	_____	16. _____

Compare your words with the spelling list. Write the words you did not know in the Corrections column. If all, or all but one, of the words are correct, the following will be some of your spelling words: **bluebird, clutter, dreadful, scribble, triplets,** and **slumber.** Write them in the Corrections column and do the Alternative Homework this week.

Sort your spelling words by the beginning blend. Write them in the glasses. Then add another word with the same blend.

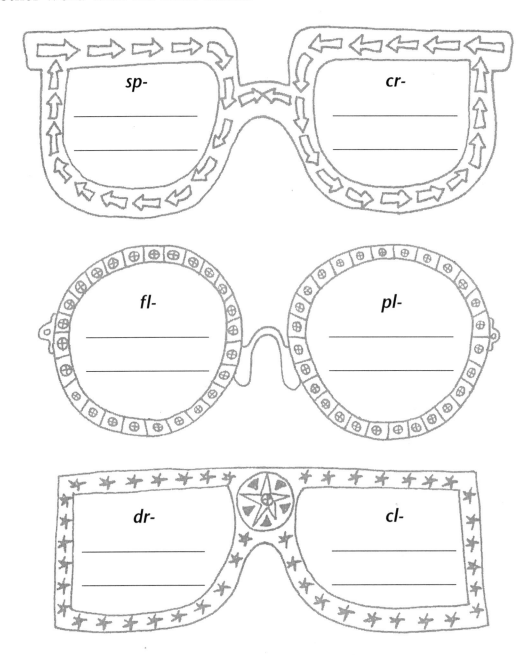

ALTERNATIVE HOMEWORK   In your reading book or textbooks find seven words with blends that you want to learn. Write these words in the Corrections column on page 1.

Make a personal spelling dictionary by folding thirteen sheets of paper in half and stapling them on the fold. Write one letter of the alphabet on the upper outside corner of each page. Then write each of your spelling words under its first letter and write a definition for it.

Write the words below under the picture of the part of the body you use to do the action. If two parts are used at the same time, write the word in both columns.

| grins   drags   slips   grabs   unstraps | | |
blew spilled trips swims claps		
		grins

Which part of the body was used most often? _____

Now write two words with blends that are not on your Spell*well* list under the headings above. If any of your Classroom Words fit, write them, too.

Write two sentences using your Classroom Words.

_____

_____

_____

Use the clues below to fill in the puzzle.

CLUES

1. It happened to your milk when you were not careful.
2. You do it when you stumble over someone's foot.
3. What you join when you become a member.
4. A terrible creature that breathes fire.
5. The color of the sky.
6. A heavenly body that moves around the sun.
7. A narrow strip of leather used to hold things together.
8. What a fish does well.

Find the Word of the Week in the shaded boxes. *Clue:* It is what you all are.

Write the Word of the Week. _____

Which spelling words were not used above?

_____   _____   _____

_____   _____   _____

_____   _____

ALTERNATIVE HOMEWORK   Draw a picture of a dragon. Then write a story about how triplets saved a friendly dragon from a dreadful hurricane.

Below are several words that are parts of spelling words. Think of a spelling word and also another word that have this word within them. Write them in the boxes above each word. You may use a dictionary. The first one is done for you.

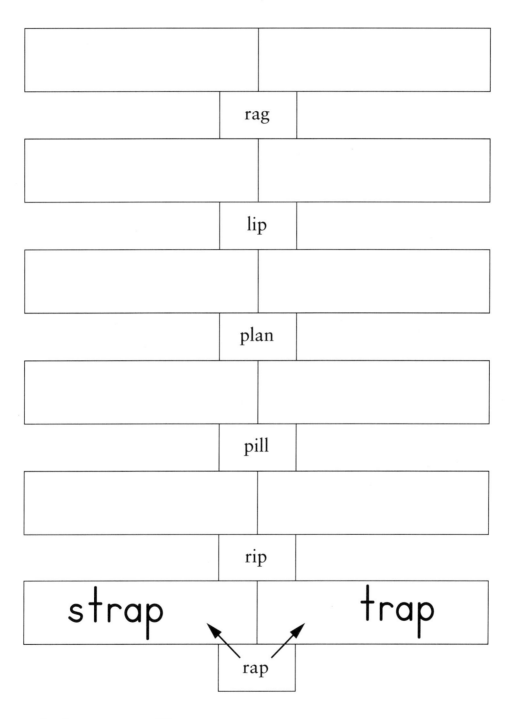

Be sure to study for your spelling test.

Copy the words your teacher gives you under Classroom Words. Fold this page back along the dotted line so that only the Pretest column shows. Write the words your teacher dictates.

Pretest	Corrections	Spell*well* Words
1. _____	_____	1. camp
2. _____	_____	2. held
3. _____	_____	3. kept
4. _____	_____	4. left
5. _____	_____	5. melt
6. _____	_____	6. print
7. _____	_____	7. spend
8. _____	_____	8. stamps
9. _____	_____	9. twist
10. _____	_____	10. subtract

Outlaw Words

11. _____	_____	11. half
12. _____	_____	12. yourself

Classroom Words

13. _____	_____	13. _____
14. _____	_____	14. _____
15. _____	_____	15. _____
16. _____	_____	16. _____

Compare your words with the spelling list. Write the words you did not know in the Corrections column. If all, or all but one, of the words are correct, the following will be some of your spelling words: **adults, erupting, wolf, subtraction, tractor,** and **yourselves.** Write them in the Corrections column and do the Alternative Homework this week.

Find a spelling word that has the same final blend as the one on the sign. Write it on the first line. Then add other words that end the same way.

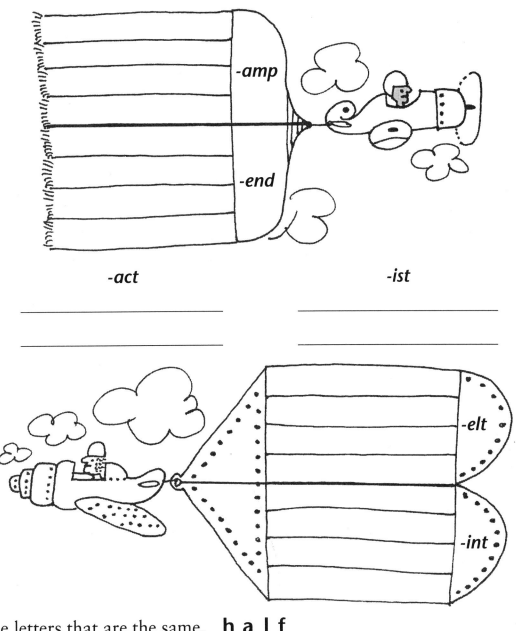

-act   *-ist*

_____   _____

_____   _____

Circle the letters that are the same. **h a l f**
                                       s e l f

One of these words has a silent letter. Underline the word and color the silent letter to help you remember it.

<u>ALTERNATIVE HOMEWORK</u>   In your reading book or textbooks find six words with final blends that you want to learn. Write these words in the Corrections column on page 6. Then write the words and their definitions in your personal dictionary.

Pick the spelling word that tells

1. what the sun will do to a snowman. _____

2. which hand you use if you don't use your right hand. _____

3. what you do with money at the store. _____

4. what you did with the money you didn't spend. _____ it

5. what you do when you take away an amount. _____

6. what you put on letters before you mail them. _____

7. what you did to the ladder so a pal could climb safely.

_____ it

8. what you do when you write a letter. _____

9. what you do when you sleep outside in a tent. _____ out

10. what you get when you share with another person. _____

Which spelling words were not used on this page? _____

_____

Choose the longest Classroom Word and make as many words as possible out of the letters.

_____

_____

ALTERNATIVE HOMEWORK   Using six of your spelling words, write a Picking Time puzzle like the one above. Be sure to write the words you use at the bottom of the page. Trade papers with another student and work each other's puzzles.

How many words can you make by adding *ing* to your spelling words? Can you reach the top rung? The first one has been done for you. You can remove any final *s* to make a word.

Write the spelling words you are not sure you know.

_____

_____

_____

_____

camping

Which word is the opposite of *right*? _____

Which means the opposite of "gave away"? _____

Which word means "you"? _____

<u>ALTERNATIVE HOMEWORK</u>   Climb the ladder using your spelling words. You may add other words if you do not have enough to reach the top.

Write a story about an elf who wants to go to camp. Tell what the elf wants to learn while at camp and how he or she will do it. Try to use six spelling words in your story. You may illustrate it if you wish.

BINGO

Your teacher will dictate your spelling words. Write one word in each box in any order you wish.

Your teacher will read the words again. Put a marker on each word you hear. When you have four in a row, say "Bingo!" If you have spelled the words correctly, you are the winner! If not, the game continues until there is a winner.

Be sure to study the words you miss for your spelling test.

ALTERNATIVE HOMEWORK   Do the activities above.

Copy the words your teacher gives you under Classroom Words. Fold this page back along the dotted line so that only the Pretest column shows. Write the words your teacher dictates.

Spell*well* Words	Corrections	Pretest
1. bang	_____	1. _____
2. belong	_____	2. _____
3. bringing	_____	3. _____
4. hunger	_____	4. _____
5. spring	_____	5. _____
6. stings	_____	6. _____
7. string	_____	7. _____
8. strong	_____	8. _____
9. something	_____	9. _____

Outlaw Words

10. wrong	_____	10. _____
11. right	_____	11. _____
12. write	_____	12. _____

Classroom Words

13. _____	_____	13. _____
14. _____	_____	14. _____
15. _____	_____	15. _____
16. _____	_____	16. _____

Compare your words with the spelling list. Write the words you did not know in the Corrections column. If all, or all but one, of the words are correct, the following will be some of your spelling words: **stringing, hungry, belongings, wrongdoing, sprang,** and **single**. Write them in the Corrections column and do the Alternative Homework this week.

1. Which spelling word ends in *er*? _____

   Add *er* to *strong, bang, sting,* and *hang.* _____

   _____   _____   _____

2. Which spelling word ends with two *ings*? _____

   Add *ing* to *wrong, string, spring,* and *belong.* _____

   _____   _____   _____

3. Add *no, some, any,* and *every* to the beginning of *thing.* _____

   _____   _____   _____

4. Add *re* to the beginning of *write, copy, string,* and *turning.*

   _____   _____   _____

   _____

5. Add *le* to the end of *sing, bang,* and *tang.*

   _____   _____   _____

6. Which spelling word means "correct"? _____

7. Which spelling word means "not correct"? _____

8. Which spelling word means "the opposite of left"? _____

9. Which spelling word means "to make letters

   with a pencil"? _____

   Add *r* to the word above to make

   another word for author. _____

ALTERNATIVE HOMEWORK   In your reading book or textbooks find six words that you want to learn. Write these words in the Corrections column on page 11. Then write the words and their definitions in your personal dictionary.

How many words can you make by adding *ing* to your spelling words? Can you reach the top rung? The first one has been done for you. You can remove any final *s* to make a word. Be sure to write the word that already has two *ing*s.

Write the spelling words you are not sure you know.

_____

_____

_____

_____

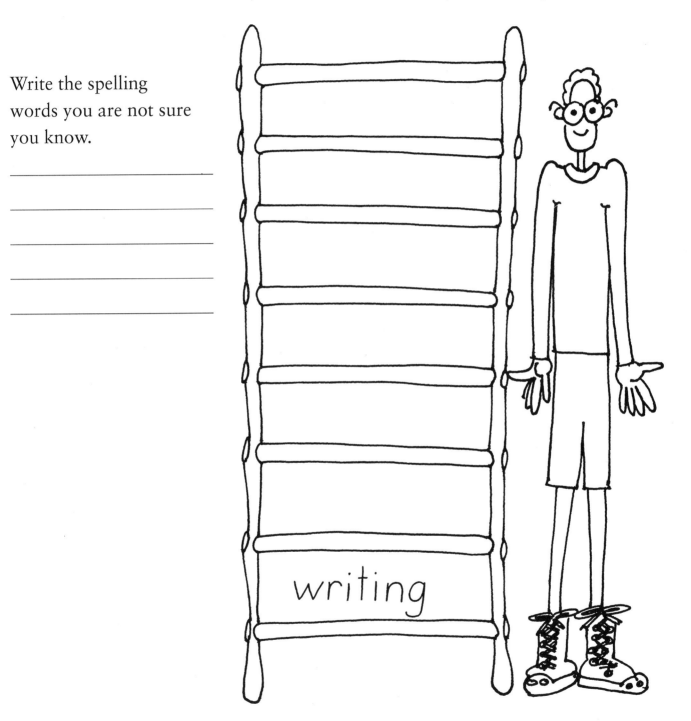

writing

<u>ALTERNATIVE HOMEWORK</u>   Draw a picture of your favorite belonging and then describe it. Be sure to tell its size, shape, color, what it is made of, what you do with it, and why it is your favorite belonging.

Write the underlined words under the picture of the part of the body you use to do the action. If two parts are used at the same time, write the word in both columns.

🦶	🖐	👄

1. <u>bangs</u> on the door

2. <u>springs</u> out of a chair

3. eats hot chili that <u>stings</u>

4. gives the <u>right</u> answer

5. puts <u>string</u> on a kite

6. kicks a <u>long</u> field goal

7. dials a <u>wrong</u> number

8. <u>sings</u> and dances to jazz

9. <u>writes</u> a long report

10. built a <u>strong</u> sandcastle

Which part of the body was used most often? _____

Which spelling words were not used on this page?

_____   _____   _____

_____   _____   _____

<u>ALTERNATIVE HOMEWORK</u>   Do the activity above. Add your own words when you can.

Find other *-ng* words in your reading book or textbooks and send them to the moon by writing them on the spaceship before it blasts off!

Write the words you
missed on the pretest.

_____

_____

_____

_____

Write your Classroom
Words in color.

_____

_____

_____

Be sure to study for your spelling test.

ALTERNATIVE HOMEWORK   Do the activity above.

Copy the words your teacher gives you under Classroom Words. Fold this page back along the dotted line so that only the Pretest column shows. Write the words your teacher dictates.

Pretest	Corrections	Spell*well* Words
1. _____	_____	1. basket
2. _____	_____	2. finger
3. _____	_____	3. happen
4. _____	_____	4. hundred
5. _____	_____	5. invent
6. _____	_____	6. monster
7. _____	_____	7. chapter
8. _____	_____	8. rubber
9. _____	_____	9. silver
10. _____	_____	10. understand
		Outlaw Words
11. _____	_____	11. before
12. _____	_____	12. four
		Classroom Words
13. _____	_____	13. _____
14. _____	_____	14. _____
15. _____	_____	15. _____
16. _____	_____	16. _____

Compare your words with the spelling list. Write the words you did not know in the Corrections column. If all, or all but one, of the words are correct, the following will be some of your spelling words: **answered, splendid, misunderstanding, silverware, wastebasket,** and **fingernails.** Write them in the Corrections column and do the Alternative Homework this week.

1. Find the spelling words that
   end in the sound of /er/ as in *her*.

   _____   _____

   _____   _____

   _____

   Which one has *er* in the middle? _____

   Write two more words that end with *er*. _____   _____

2. One spelling word is a compound word (two words put together).

   Which word is compound? _____

   Write two more compound words that include a spelling word.

   _____   _____

3. Find the spelling words that name numbers.

   _____   _____

4. Find the spelling word that means "ahead of" or "in front of."

   _____

5. Find the spelling word that has *ask* in it. _____

6. Find the spelling word that means "to make up" or "to think of something

   new." _____

7. Find the spelling word that ends with the name of something you write with.

   _____

8. Find the spelling words that were not used above. _____

   _____

   _____

ALTERNATIVE HOMEWORK   In your reading book or textbooks find six words with
er that you want to learn. Write these words in the Corrections column on page 16.
Then write the words and their definitions in your personal dictionary.

Write a spelling word on each line.

1. Not eggs in a box, but eggs in a _____

2. Not ten dimes, but a _____ pennies

3. Not one page, but a _____

4. Not gold, but _____

5. Not your toe, but your _____

6. Not after, but _____

7. Not an elastic band, but a _____ band

8. Not a vampire, but a _____

9. Not three, but _____

Write the small words you see in these words.

happen _____   muffin _____

finger _____   summer _____

better _____   lesson _____

Write the small words you see in your Classroom Words.

_____

_____

ALTERNATIVE HOMEWORK   How many words of three or more letters can you find hidden in your spelling words? Write them. The student with the most correct words wins.

Write the spelling word that fits the category. Then write another word (not in the lesson) that also fits the category.

1. **Stretchy things:** elastic, sweater, ___rubber___ band, ___suspenders___

2. **Parts of a book:** index, title page, _____ , _____

3. **Parts of the body:** head, foot, _____ , _____

4. **Metals:** copper, iron, _____ , _____

5. **Words that tell when:** after, earlier, _____ , _____

6. **Used to hold or carry things:** bag, box, _____ , _____

7. **Big numbers:** thousand, fifty, _____ , _____

8. **Scary things:** witch, vampire, _____ , _____

9. **One-digit numerals:** one, two, _____ , _____

Make new words by adding *ing* to some of your spelling words.

_____   _____   _____

Add *ing* to some of your Classroom Words or write other two-syllable words that end in *ing*.

_____   _____   _____

Write sentences using some of your Classroom Words.

_____

_____

ALTERNATIVE HOMEWORK   Do the activity above.

Find other two-syllable words in your reading book or textbooks and send them to the moon by writing them on the spaceship before it blasts off!

Write the words you
missed on the pretest.

_____

_____

_____

_____

Add *s*, *ed*, or *er*
to as many Classroom
Words as possible.

_____

_____

_____

_____

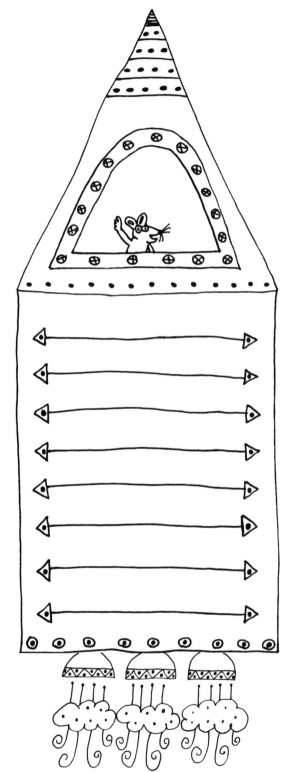

Be sure to study for your spelling test.

ALTERNATIVE HOMEWORK   Do the activity above.

Copy the words your teacher gives you under Classroom Words. Fold this page back along the dotted line so that only the Pretest column shows. Write the words your teacher dictates.

Spell*well* Words	Corrections	Pretest
1. broke	_____	1. _____
2. close	_____	2. _____
3. drive	_____	3. _____
4. invite	_____	4. _____
5. mistake	_____	5. _____
6. notebook	_____	6. _____
7. skates	_____	7. _____
8. suppose	_____	8. _____
9. tire	_____	9. _____
10. use	_____	10. _____
11. hole	_____	11. _____

Outlaw Words

| 12. whole | _____ | 12. _____ |

Classroom Words

13. _____	_____	13. _____
14. _____	_____	14. _____
15. _____	_____	15. _____
16. _____	_____	16. _____

Compare your words with the spelling list. Write the words you did not know in the Corrections column. If all, or all but one, of the words are correct, the following will be some of your spelling words: **wholesome, bulldozer, complete, daredevil, profile,** and **vampire.** Write them in the Corrections column and do the Alternative Homework this week.

Sort your spelling words by their vowel sounds and write them in the barrels. Then write other words that follow the same pattern of vowel, consonant, and silent *e* next to the arrows.

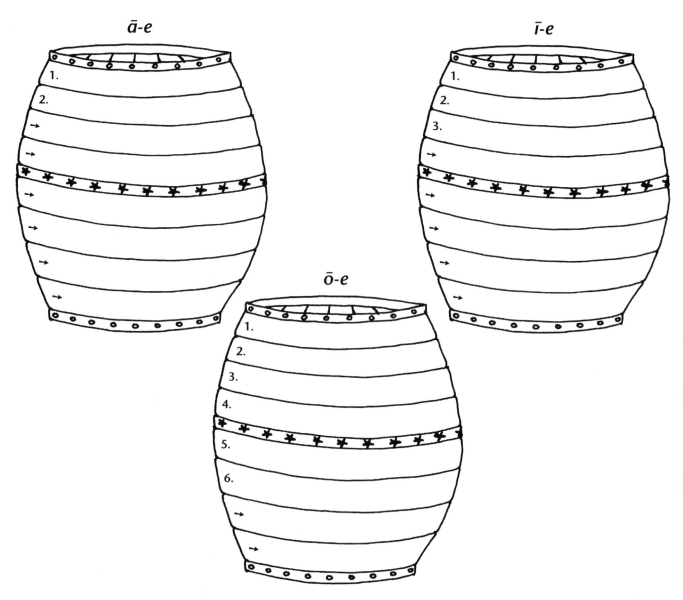

Rule: When you hear a long-vowel sound, it may be spelled by a vowel, followed by a consonant and the letter ____. The *e* is silent, but it makes the vowel say its

_____.

ALTERNATIVE HOMEWORK   In your reading book or textbooks find six words that end with silent *e* that you want to learn. Write these words in the Corrections column on page 21. Then write the words and their definitions in your personal dictionary.

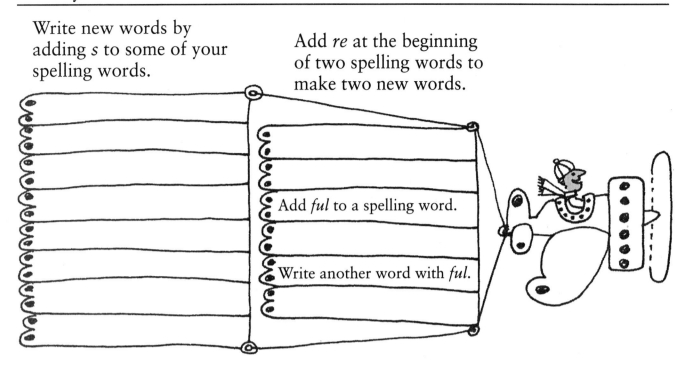

Write new words by adding *s* to some of your spelling words.

Add *re* at the beginning of two spelling words to make two new words.

Add *ful* to a spelling word.

Write another word with *ful*.

Add a spelling word to the words below. Then write the compound words next to their parts.

1. _____ + way   = _____

2. _____ + some   = _____

3. house + _____n   = _____

4. over + _____   = _____

5. _____ + less   = _____

Write your Classroom Words and their definitions.

_____

_____

_____

_____

ALTERNATIVE HOMEWORK   Write your ten hardest spelling words on the sky signs above. Add endings to them if you can.

Write the underlined words under the picture of the part of the body you use to do the action. If two parts are used at the same time, write the word in both columns.

👣	✋	👄

1. <u>invites</u> a pal overnight

2. <u>closes</u> the lid

3. <u>drives</u> a jeep

4. <u>broke</u> a bottle

5. <u>uses</u> a jump rope

6. makes a <u>mistake</u> counting

7. changes a flat <u>tire</u>

8. writes in a <u>notebook</u>

9. <u>skates</u> on the pond

10. <u>broke</u> the tie in a game

Can you add any Classroom Words?

11. _____

12. _____

Which part of the body was used most often? _____

Write your Classroom Words from longest to shortest.

_____

_____

<u>ALTERNATIVE HOMEWORK</u>   Do the activity above. Add your own words when you can.

Write a story about something important that has happened or might happen to you this year. Try to use five spelling words in your story. You may illustrate it if you wish.

BINGO

Your teacher will dictate your spelling words. Write one word in each box in any order you wish.

Your teacher will read the words again. Put a marker on each word you hear. When you have four in a row, say "Bingo!" If you have spelled the words correctly, you are the winner! If not, the game continues until there is a winner.

Be sure to study the words you miss for your spelling test.

ALTERNATIVE HOMEWORK   Do the activities above.

Copy the words your teacher gives you under Classroom Words. Fold this page back along the dotted line so that only the Pretest column shows. Write the words your teacher dictates.

Pretest	Corrections	Spell*well* Words
1. _____	_____	1. almost
2. _____	_____	2. behind
3. _____	_____	3. golden
4. _____	_____	4. mind
5. _____	_____	5. oldest
6. _____	_____	6. pint
7. _____	_____	7. poster
8. _____	_____	8. scold
9. _____	_____	9. unkind
10. _____	_____	10. wild
		Outlaw Words
11. _____	_____	11. comb
12. _____	_____	12. climb
		Classroom Words
13. _____	_____	13. _____
14. _____	_____	14. _____
15. _____	_____	15. _____
16. _____	_____	16. _____

Compare your words with the spelling list. Write the words you did not know in the Corrections column. If all, or all but one, of the words are correct, the following will be some of your spelling words: **blindfold, candleholder, mildness, soldier, reminder,** and **postpone.** Write them in the Corrections column and do the Alternative Homework this week.

Write spelling words that rhyme and circle the letters that are alike. You may drop any ending (*en, er, est*). Then add another word that rhymes. Remember, when words rhyme they have the same vowel sound and the same last consonant.

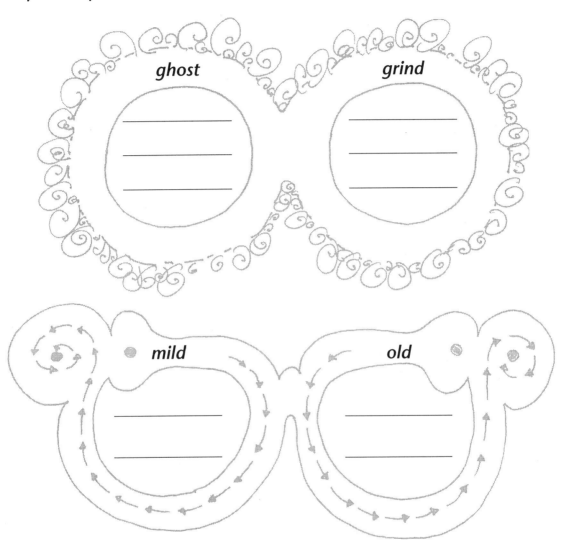

ghost

grind

mild

old

Using all of the words above and the rest of your spelling words, make new words by adding *er*. (Don't forget the one that already ends in *er*.)

_____   _____   _____

_____   _____   _____

_____

<u>ALTERNATIVE HOMEWORK</u>   In your reading book or textbooks find six more words that you want to learn. Write these words in the Corrections column on page 26. Then write the words and their definitions in your personal dictionary.

1. Pick the spelling word that means "mean and bad." _____

2. Pick the one you use on your hair. _____

3. Pick the one that has lived a long time. _____

4. Pick the one that is needed to think with. _____

5. Pick the one that is not tame. _____

6. Pick the one that can be hung on a wall. _____

7. Pick the one that describes a crown. _____

8. Pick the one 2 hands and 2 feet can do. _____

9. Pick the size of container that cream comes in.

_____

10. Pick the one that is slow in a race. _____

11. Pick the one that means "nearly." _____

12. Pick the one that tells what you do when your dog is bad.

_____

Write your Classroom Words. _____

_____

_____

ALTERNATIVE HOMEWORK   Draw a picture of a goldfish or a wildcat. Give your picture a title. On the back write all the words that describe your creature and where it lives. Can you use any of your spelling words?

Write the spelling word that fits the category. Then write another word (not in the lesson) that also fits the category.

1. **Words that describe jewelry:** silvery, pearl, _____ , _____

2. **Ways to move:** crawl, jog, _____ , _____

3. **Words about age:** elderly, babyish, _____ , _____

4. **Things to hang on a wall:** map, picture, _____ , _____

5. **Bad behavior in class:** loud, sassy, _____ , _____

6. **Used in the hair:** bow, barrette, _____ , _____

7. **Liquid measures:** cup, gallon, _____ , _____

OPPOSITES / DIFFERENCES

Write a word that is the opposite of or different in meaning from each word below. The last four words with * are *not* spelling words, but they follow the same spelling pattern.

1. tame ⟷ _____   6. slide down ⟷ _____ up

2. ahead ⟷ _____   *7. adult ⟷ _____

3. youngest ⟷ _____   *8. lose ⟷ _____

4. praise ⟷ _____   *9. hot ⟷ _____

5. kind ⟷ _____   *10. mean ⟷ _____

Add *s*, *ed*, or *er* to your Classroom Words. If you cannot, just write the word.

_____   _____   _____

_____

ALTERNATIVE HOMEWORK   Do the activities above.

Below are several spelling words or parts of spelling words. Think of other words that are related or have this word within them. Write them in the boxes above each word. You may use a dictionary.

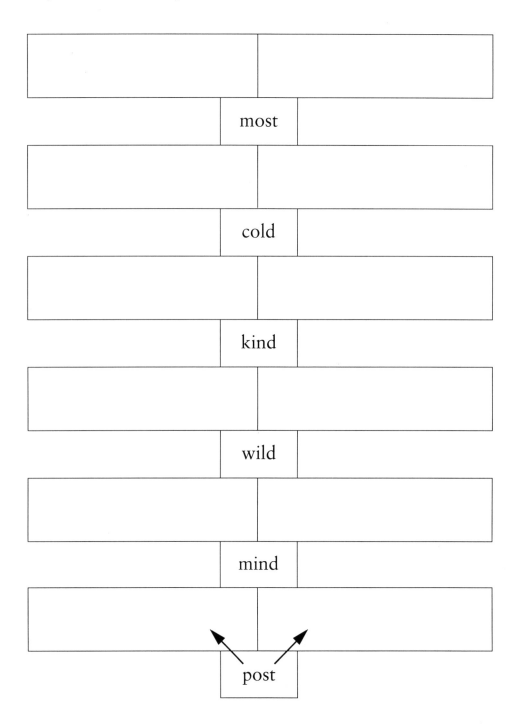

Be sure to study for your spelling test.

<u>ALTERNATIVE HOMEWORK</u>   Do the activity above.

Copy the words your teacher gives you under Classroom Words. Fold this page back along the dotted line so that only the Pretest column shows. Cover page 33 so you cannot see it. Write the words your teacher dictates.

Spell*well* Words	Corrections	Pretest
1. brush	_____	1. _____
2. dishpan	_____	2. _____
3. flash	_____	3. _____
4. freshest	_____	4. _____
5. shed	_____	5. _____
6. selfish	_____	6. _____
7. ship	_____	7. _____
8. shade	_____	8. _____
9. smash	_____	9. _____
10. finish	_____	10. _____

Outlaw Words

11. full	_____	11. _____
12. pull	_____	12. _____
13. push	_____	13. _____

Classroom Words

14. _____	_____	14. _____
15. _____	_____	15. _____
16. _____	_____	16. _____

Compare your words with the spelling list. Write the words you did not know in the Corrections column. If all, or all but one, of the words are correct, the following will be some of your spelling words: **dishwasher, flashlight, hairbrush, toolshed, shipwreck,** and **vanished.** Write them in the Corrections column and do the Alternative Homework this week.

1. Find a compound word that tells what you need

   to wash dishes. _____

2. Find the spelling words that have
   the word *ash* in them.

   _____　_____

   Write another word with *ash* in it.　_____

3. Find a spelling word that has a word in it that tells a part of the body.

   _____

4. Find the spelling word that has in it a little word that means "to hurry" or "to

   move fast." _____

5. Find the spelling word that tells about someone who doesn't share.

   _____

6. Find the spelling word that begins with a word that names part of a fish's body.

   _____

7. Find other words hidden in your spelling words. Write the spelling words and
   circle the little words in them.

   _____　_____　_____

   _____　_____　_____

   _____　_____　_____

8. Find two spelling words that rhyme.　_____　_____

9. Find the spelling word that means "to shove."　_____

ALTERNATIVE HOMEWORK　　　In your reading book or textbooks find seven words
that you want to learn. Write these words in the Corrections column on page 31.
Then write the words and their definitions in your personal dictionary.

Find the spelling words pictured in the scene below. Draw an arrow to the part of the picture that represents the word. Then write the spelling words on the lines.

1. _____
2. _____
3. _____
4. _____
5. _____
6. _____
7. _____

Write two spelling words that are opposite in meaning. (They tell about moving a

heavy thing.) _____   _____

Write the spelling words with double *l*.

_____   _____

Which spelling words were not used on this page?

_____

_____

Scramble the letters of your Classroom Words on the top lines. Trade papers with another student and unscramble each other's words.

_____ _____ _____

_____ _____ _____

ALTERNATIVE HOMEWORK   How many words can you make using the root *ship*? You may add letters at the beginning or end. Use a dictionary if you get stuck. Can you find seven words? Write them on the lines next to the picture above.

Write a spelling word on each line.

1. Not in the sun, but in the _____

2. Not a fry pan, but a _____

3. Not start a job, but _____ it

4. Not a rowboat, but a large _____

5. Not empty, but _____

6. Not a comb, but a _____

7. Not a big barn, but a little _____

8. Not a candle, but a _____ light

9. Not stalest, but _____

10. Not push the wagon, but _____ it

Which spelling words were not used?

_____

_____

Write your Classroom Words from shortest to longest.

_____

_____

ALTERNATIVE HOMEWORK   Using six of your spelling words, write a Use Your Head puzzle like the one above. Be sure to write the words you use at the bottom of the page. Trade papers with another student and work each other's puzzles.

How many words can you make by adding another word to a spelling word or part of a spelling word? Can you reach the top rung? The first one has been done for you. You may use a dictionary.

Write the spelling
words you are not sure
you know.

_____

_____

_____

_____

friendship

Be sure to study for your spelling test.

<u>ALTERNATIVE HOMEWORK</u>   Do the activity above.

Copy the words your teacher gives you under Classroom Words. Fold this page back along the dotted line so that only the Pretest column shows. Write the words your teacher dictates.

Pretest	Corrections	Spell*well* Words
1. _____	_____	1. catch
2. _____	_____	2. champ
3. _____	_____	3. chest
4. _____	_____	4. children
5. _____	_____	5. chill
6. _____	_____	6. chin
7. _____	_____	7. chips
8. _____	_____	8. hatch
9. _____	_____	9. inch
10. _____	_____	10. kitchen
11. _____	_____	11. lunch
		Outlaw Words
12. _____	_____	12. goes
13. _____	_____	13. says
		Classroom Words
14. _____	_____	14. _____
15. _____	_____	15. _____
16. _____	_____	16. _____

Compare your words with the spelling list. Write the words you did not know in the Corrections column. If all, or all but one, of the words are correct, the following will be some of your spelling words: **channel, chopsticks, touchdown, chipmunk, coach,** and **hitchhike.** Write them in the Corrections column and do the Alternative Homework this week.

Write the spelling word that tells

1. what you do when a pal throws a ball. _____

2. what you eat at noon. _____

3. what youngsters are called. _____

4. what you do to jello. _____

5. what eggs sometimes do. _____

6. where you prepare food. _____

7. what the winner is sometimes called. _____

8. what treasure can be found in. _____

9. what the lower part of your jaw is called. _____

Write the spelling words that are opposite in meaning.

1. adults _____   3. throw _____

2. comes _____   4. heat _____

Notice: Sometimes words are pronounced differently when they add *s*. For example, When I *say* "How are you?" he *says* "Fine." Do the words *say* and *says* sound alike? _____

The /z/ sound in *says* is spelled with the letter ____. You also hear /z/ at the end of *goes*. For example, I *go* to school by bus, but my friend *goes* by car. The /z/ sound in *goes* is spelled with the letters ____ ____.

ALTERNATIVE HOMEWORK   In your reading book or textbooks find seven words with *ch* that you want to learn. Write these words in the Corrections column on page 36. Then write the words and their definitions in your personal dictionary.

Find the spelling words pictured in the scene below. Draw an arrow to the part of the picture that represents the word. Then write the spelling words on the lines.

1. _____
2. _____
3. _____
4. _____
5. _____
6. _____

Which Spell*well* Words are not pictured?

_____

_____

What do you think will happen next in the picture? _____

_____

_____

Which Spell*well* Word tells where the children should eat their lunch?

_____

Write three sentences using your Classroom Words.

_____

_____

_____

ALTERNATIVE HOMEWORK   How many other *ch* and *tch* words can you think of? Do *not* use the words on page 36. You are a champ if you can write twenty words.

Use the clues to fill in the puzzle.

CLUES

1. The winner of a match.
2. Twelve of these make one foot.
3. The front of the jaw.
4. A place to cook and prepare food.
5. The noon meal.
6. People younger than adults.
7. Treasure might be found in it.

Find the Word of the Week in the shaded boxes. *Clue:* You can draw this.

Write the Word of the Week. _____

Remember: Sometimes the /z/ sound is spelled with the letter _____. Sometimes the /z/ sound is spelled with the letters _____ _____.

Do the Outlaw Words rhyme? _____ Write them. _____ _____

Write the Outlaw Words in the sentences.
I say "Hello," and she _____ "Hi."
When I go to the store, my friend _____ with me.

Write your Classroom Words and their definitions.

_____

_____

_____

ALTERNATIVE HOMEWORK   How many new words can you make by adding an ending or prefix to the Spell*well* Words on page 36? Write the new words.

Write a story about a champ (or a chimp) and something very special that he, she, or it did. Be sure your story has a beginning, a middle, and an end. Try to use at least four spelling words in your story. You may illustrate it if you wish.

BINGO

Your teacher will dictate your spelling words. Write one word in each box in any order you wish.

Your teacher will read the words again. Put a marker on each word you hear. When you have four in a row, say "Bingo!" If you have spelled the words correctly, you are the winner! If not, the game continues until there is a winner.

Be sure to study the words you miss for your spelling test.

<u>ALTERNATIVE HOMEWORK</u>   Do the activities above.

Copy the words your teacher gives you under Classroom Words. Fold this page back along the dotted line so that only the Pretest column shows. Write the words your teacher dictates.

Spell*well* Words	Corrections	Pretest
1. bathtub	_____	1. _____
2. math	_____	2. _____
3. sixth	_____	3. _____
4. thrill	_____	4. _____
5. these	_____	5. _____
6. whale	_____	6. _____
7. whine	_____	7. _____
8. whip	_____	8. _____
9. whisper	_____	9. _____
10. without	_____	10. _____

Outlaw Words

11. other	_____	11. _____
12. another	_____	12. _____

Classroom Words

13. _____	_____	13. _____
14. _____	_____	14. _____
15. _____	_____	15. _____
16. _____	_____	16. _____

Compare your words with the spelling list. Write the words you did not know in the Corrections column. If all, or all but one, of the words are correct, the following will be some of your spelling words: **arithmetic, athlete, otherwise, ninth, whining,** and **filthy.** Write them in the Corrections column and do the Alternative Homework this week.

Write a spelling word that rhymes and circle the letters that are alike. Then add another word that rhymes.

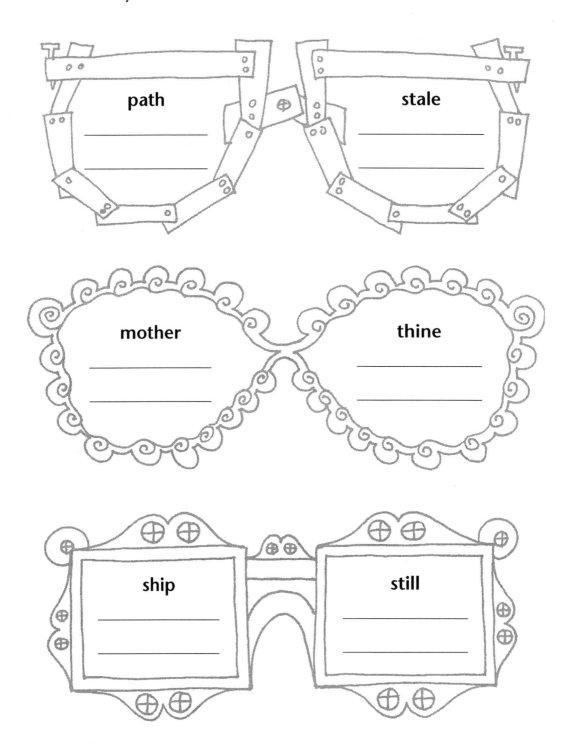

path _____ _____

stale _____ _____

mother _____ _____

thine _____ _____

ship _____ _____

still _____ _____

ALTERNATIVE HOMEWORK   In your reading book or textbooks find six words that you want to learn. Write these words in the Corrections column on page 41. Then write the words and their definitions in your personal dictionary.

1. Pick the biggest mammal. _____

2. Pick the one you study in school. _____

3. Pick the one dogs do when they are sad. _____

4. Pick the one that describes a shivery feeling. _____

5. Pick the one you might do to cream. _____

6. Pick the one you do when you tell a secret. _____

7. Pick the one that comes after fifth. _____

8. Pick the one that holds water. _____

9. Pick the word you use when asking a question about a choice.

   You might ask, "Do you want *those* or _____?"

Questions often begin with *wh* words. Think of some *wh* words used in questions.

   1. Pick the one that asks about a reason for something.

      _____ do you like snakes?

   2. Pick the one that asks about a time.

      _____ are you going to leave?

   3. Pick the one that asks about a choice between two things.

      _____ of these do you like best?

      Add *s*, *ed*, or *er* to your Classroom Words if possible. _____

      _____

ALTERNATIVE HOMEWORK   Using six of your spelling words, write a Picking Time puzzle like the one above. Be sure to write the words you use at the bottom of the page. Trade papers with another student and work each other's puzzles.

Write the Spell*well* Word that is opposite.

1. shout to a pal ←—→ _____ to a pal

2. a tiny minnow ←—→ a huge _____

3. with help ←—→ _____ help

The next ones are *not* opposites, but go together in some way.
Write the Spell*well* Word that fits.

4. stir the soup —→ _____ the cream

5. wade in a mud puddle —→ soak in the _____

6. cat's meow —→ dog's _____

7. the grade before seventh —→ _____

The next words are spelled with *th* or *wh*. They are opposites but are *not* spelling words.

8. fat cat ←—→ _____ cat

9. us ←—→ _____

10. black ←—→ _____

11. drive on a city highway ←—→ walk on a woodsy _____

Write the two Outlaw Words and then write another word that rhymes.

_____   _____   _____

Which spelling words were not used on this page?

_____

_____

ALTERNATIVE HOMEWORK   Do the activity on this page.

Write a story about a whale that got lost at sea. Try to use five spelling words in your story. Be sure to tell what happened, when and where it happened, and why. You may illustrate it if you wish.

BINGO

Your teacher will dictate your spelling words. Write one word in each box in any order you wish.

Your teacher will read the words again. Put a marker on each word you hear. When you have four in a row, say "Bingo!" If you have spelled the words correctly, you are the winner! If not, the game continues until there is a winner.

Be sure to study the words you miss for your spelling test.

ALTERNATIVE HOMEWORK   Do the activities above.

Copy the words your teacher gives you under Classroom Words. Fold this page back along the dotted line so that only the Pretest column shows. Write the words your teacher dictates.

Pretest	Corrections	Spell*well* Words
1. _____	_____	1. batting
2. _____	_____	2. beginning
3. _____	_____	3. clapped
4. _____	_____	4. digging
5. _____	_____	5. dropped
6. _____	_____	6. planned
7. _____	_____	7. rubbed
8. _____	_____	8. setting
9. _____	_____	9. shopping
10. _____	_____	10. stepped
		Outlaw Words
11. _____	_____	11. true
12. _____	_____	12. truly
		Classroom Words
13. _____	_____	13. _____
14. _____	_____	14. _____
15. _____	_____	15. _____
16. _____	_____	16. _____

Compare your words with the spelling list. Write the words you did not know in the Corrections column. If all, or all but one, of the words are correct, the following will be some of your spelling words: **collected, prodded, expected, seeking, unforgettable,** and **upsetting.** Write them in the Corrections column and do the Alternative Homework this week.

Sort your spelling words by their endings and write them in the barrels.

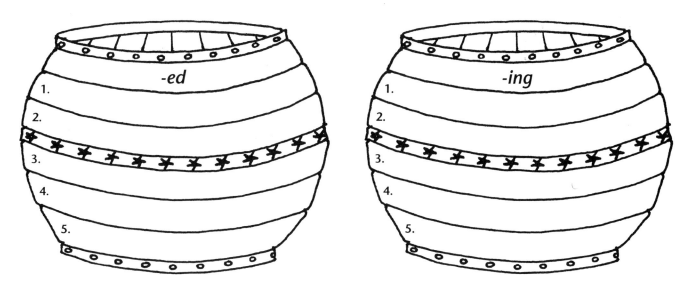

Circle the root of each spelling word. Are the vowels long or short? _____
What happens to the last letter of the root when *ing* or *ed* is added?

_____

Rule: If the vowel in the root of a word is a _____ vowel with one
consonant after it, you _____ the consonant before you add *ing* or *ed*.

Add *ing* to these words.   Add *ed* to these words.

1. get _____   4. trap _____

2. hug _____   5. skip _____

3. pop _____   6. brag _____

Notice: What happens to the *e* of *true* when you add *ly*? _____
Write both Outlaw Words. _____ _____

<u>ALTERNATIVE HOMEWORK</u>   In your reading book or textbooks find six more words end-
ing with *ing* or *ed* that you want to learn. Write these words in the Corrections column
on page 46. Then write the words and their definitions in your personal dictionary.

Write the spelling word that is opposite.

1. _____ ◄─► false

2. _____ the hole ◄─► filling in the hole

3. _____ the race ◄─► ending the race

The next ones are *not* opposites but go together in some way. Write the spelling word that fits.

4. Pitching to home plate ──► _____ at home plate

5. _____ the glass vase ──► picked up the broken glass

6. Patted with a powder puff ──► _____ with a towel

7. Listened during the concert ──► _____ afterwards

8. _____ up onto the bus ──► jumped down from the bus

9. Putting money in the bank ──► _____ at the mall

10. _____ to come home ──► stayed overnight

11. Signs a letter Love and Kisses ──► signs a letter Yours _____

Copy your Classroom Words in order of size, starting with the shortest word.

_____

_____

Write the Spell*well* Word that rhymes; then write another rhyming word.

mopping   napped   netting

_____   _____   _____

_____   _____   _____

ALTERNATIVE HOMEWORK   Write a short story about your most unforgettable day. Tell what you did, what happened, and how you felt about it. Try to use some spelling words in your story.

Use the clues below to fill in the puzzle.

CLUES

1. Opposite of false.
2. Swinging at and hitting a baseball.
3. Scooping and shoveling.
4. Thought about ahead of time.
5. Polished or scrubbed by hand.
6. Going to stores to buy things.
7. Exactly; really.
8. Slapped your hands together loudly.
9. The time and place of a story.
10. Walked carefully.

Find the Word of the Week in the shaded boxes. *Clue:* We hope you do this.

Write the Word of the Week._____

Which spelling words were not used above? _____

_____

Choose the longest Classroom Word and make as many words as possible out of the letters. _____

ALTERNATIVE HOMEWORK   How many words of three or more letters can you find hidden in your spelling words? The student with the most correct words wins.

Below are several spelling words or parts of spelling words. Think of other words that are related or have this word within them. Write them in the boxes above each word. You may use a dictionary.

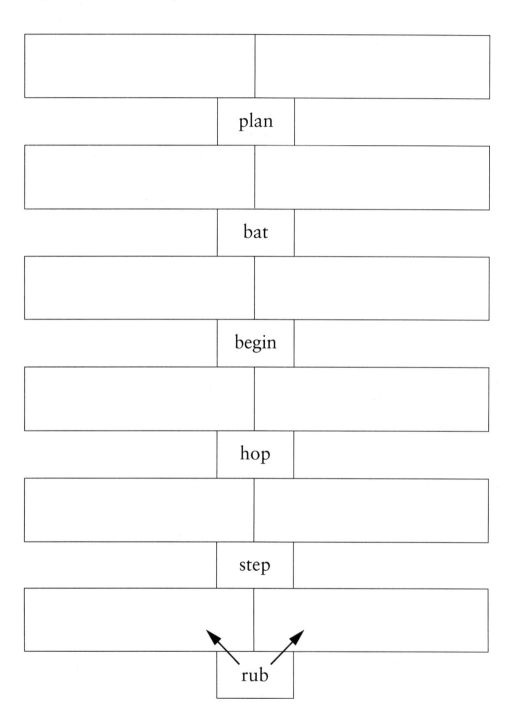

Be sure to study for your spelling test.

ALTERNATIVE HOMEWORK   Do the activity above.

Copy the words your teacher gives you under Classroom Words. Fold this page back along the dotted line so that only the Pretest column shows. Write the words your teacher dictates.

Spell*well* Words	Corrections	Pretest
1. body	_____	1. _____
2. copy	_____	2. _____
3. family	_____	3. _____
4. fuzzy	_____	4. _____
5. jelly	_____	5. _____
6. lazy	_____	6. _____
7. penny	_____	7. _____
8. silly	_____	8. _____
9. study	_____	9. _____

Outlaw Words

10. pretty	_____	10. _____
11. anybody	_____	11. _____
12. anything	_____	12. _____

Classroom Words

13. _____	_____	13. _____
14. _____	_____	14. _____
15. _____	_____	15. _____
16. _____	_____	16. _____

Compare your words with the spelling list. Write the words you did not know in the Corrections column. If all, or all but one, of the words are correct, the following will be some of your spelling words: **lazily, silliness, families, allergy, pantry,** and **satisfactory.** Write them in the Corrections column and do the Alternative Homework this week.

Write a spelling word that rhymes and circle the letters that are alike. Then add another word that rhymes.

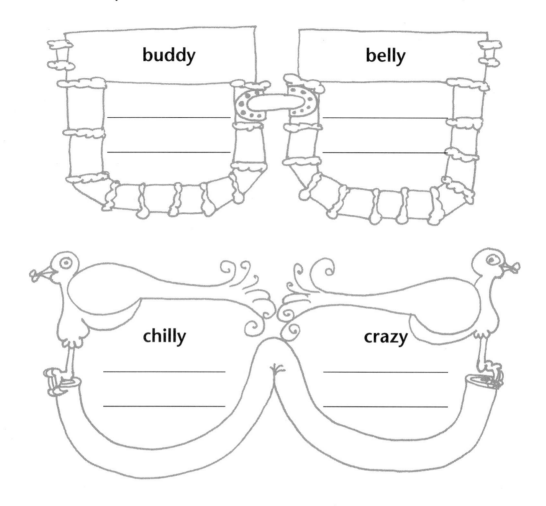

Circle a part of a spelling word in each sentence below. Then write the spelling word on the line. The first one is done for you.

1. A tool for writing is a (pen.)

   penny

2. A sill is part of a window.

   _____

3. A peach is covered with fuzz.

   _____

4. The body is the main part of a thing.

   _____

ALTERNATIVE HOMEWORK   In your reading book or textbooks find six more words with final *y* that you want to learn. Write these words in the Corrections column on page 51. Then write the words and their definitions in your personal dictionary.

Write the spelling word that names or tells

1. what goes with peanut butter. _____

2. a coin. _____

3. what to do with spelling words before a test.

_____

4. someone who does whatever another does:

a _____ cat.

5. a group of people related to one another. _____

6. the main part of a person. _____

Write two spelling words that are compound words.

_____

Write the spelling word that describes

7. a rosy sunset. _____

8. a teddy bear. _____

9. a giggling student. _____

10. someone who does no work. _____

Write your Classroom Words from shortest to longest.

_____

_____

ALTERNATIVE HOMEWORK   Draw a picture of the silliest thing you can imagine. Then describe it. Be sure to tell about the size, shape, color, texture, and its movements, if any. Finally, name it and tell its purpose.

Find the spelling words pictured in the scene below. Draw an arrow to the part of the picture that represents the word. Then write the spelling words on the lines.

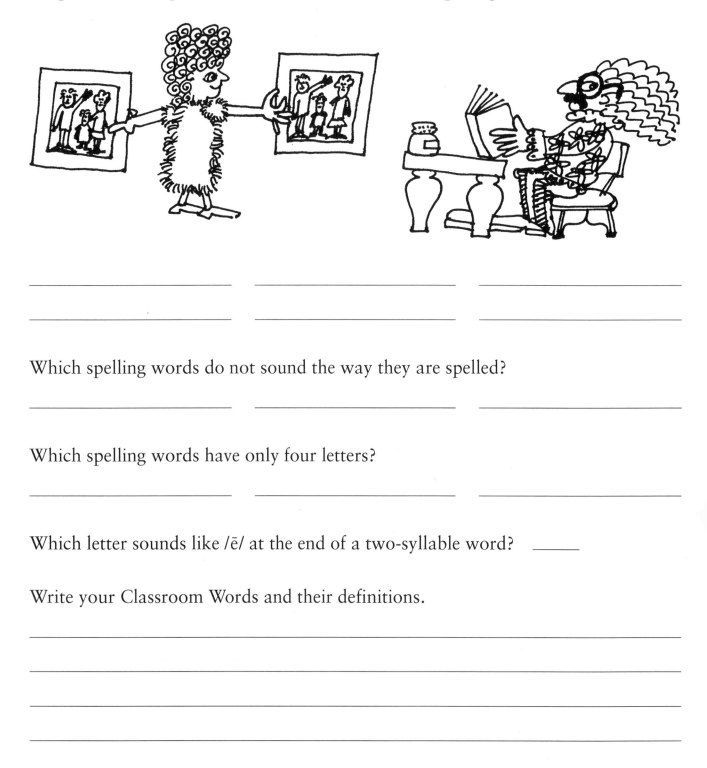

_____   _____   _____

_____   _____   _____

Which spelling words do not sound the way they are spelled?

_____   _____   _____

Which spelling words have only four letters?

_____   _____   _____

Which letter sounds like /ē/ at the end of a two-syllable word? _____

Write your Classroom Words and their definitions.

_____

_____

_____

_____

ALTERNATIVE HOMEWORK   How many words of three or more letters can you find hidden in your spelling words? Write them.

Below are several spelling words or parts of spelling words. Think of other words that are related or have this word within them. Write them in the boxes above each word. Do not use a word more than once. You may use a dictionary.

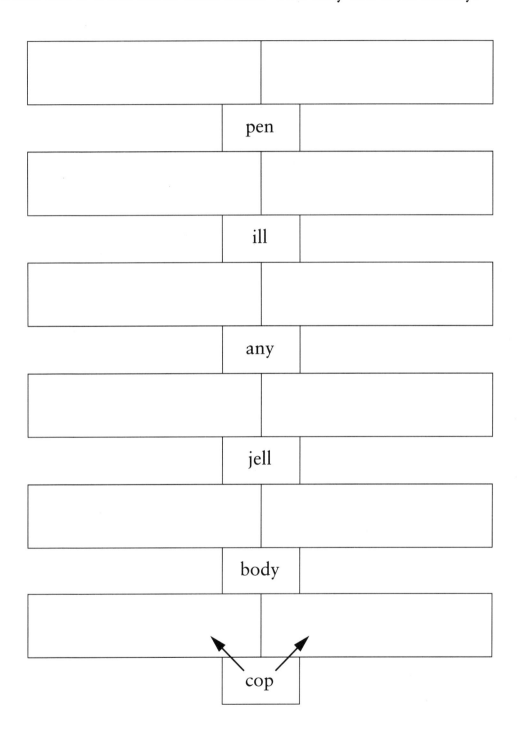

Be sure to study for your spelling test.

Copy the words your teacher gives you under Classroom Words. Fold this page back along the dotted line so that only the Pretest column shows. Write the words your teacher dictates.

Pretest	Corrections	Spell*well* Words
1. _____	_____	1. carrying
2. _____	_____	2. crying
3. _____	_____	3. diving
4. _____	_____	4. emptying
5. _____	_____	5. shining
6. _____	_____	6. skating
7. _____	_____	7. staying
8. _____	_____	8. waking
9. _____	_____	9. worrying
10. _____	_____	10. writing

Outlaw Words

11. _____	_____	11. buying
12. _____	_____	12. because

Classroom Words

13. _____	_____	13. _____
14. _____	_____	14. _____
15. _____	_____	15. _____
16. _____	_____	16. _____

Compare your words with the spelling list. Write the words you did not know in the Corrections column. If all, or all but one, of the words are correct, the following will be some of your spelling words: **chasing, obeying, surprising, frustrating, locating,** and **repaying.** Write them in the Corrections column and do the Alternative Homework this week.

Look at words 1–11 on page 56. Draw a line before the *-ing* to find each root. Some roots end with *-y* and some have dropped the final *e*. Sort the spelling words by their roots and write them in the barrels. The first one is done for you.

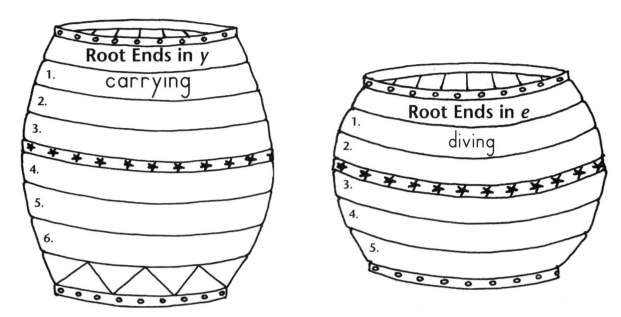

Look at the spelling words above. When a root (like dive) ends in *e*, what happens

to the *e* when you add *ing*? _____

When a word (like carry) ends in *y*, what do you do with *y* when you add *ing*?

_____

Add *ing* to these words using the rules above to help you.

1. copy + ing = _____   3. become + ing = _____

2. write + ing = _____   4. marry + ing = _____

Which spelling words were not used on this page?

_____

_____

ALTERNATIVE HOMEWORK   In your reading book or textbooks find six more words ending with *y* or silent *e* that you want to learn. Add an ending such as *-ing* to each word. Write these words in the Corrections column on page 56. Then write the words and their definitions in your personal dictionary.

Write a spelling word that rhymes and circle the letters that are alike. Then add another word that rhymes.

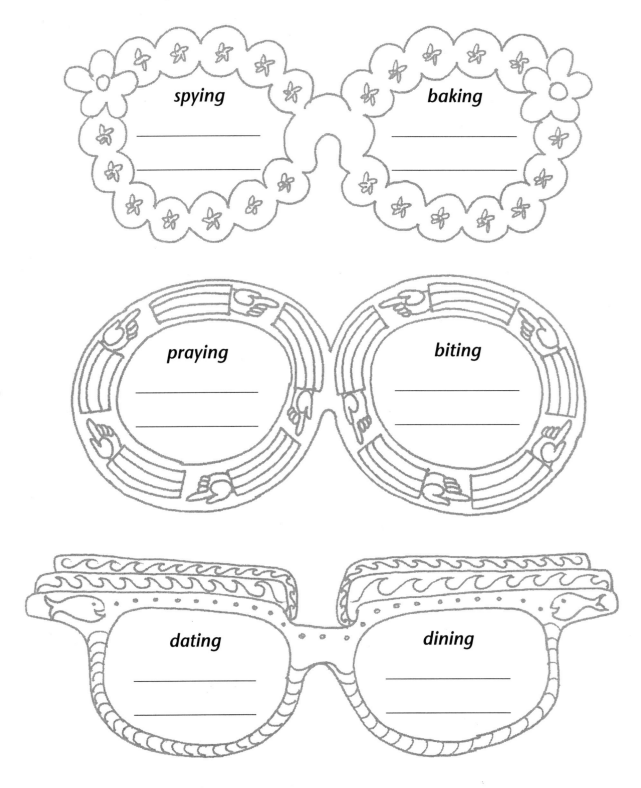

spying

baking

praying

biting

dating

dining

<u>ALTERNATIVE HOMEWORK</u>   Draw a picture of something that would scare your friend. Then describe what it looks like, how it moves, and what makes it scary.

Write the spelling word that tells

1. what you are doing on an icy pond. _____

2. what you are doing when moving a suitcase. _____

3. what you might be doing after you get hurt. _____

4. what you are doing on these lines. _____

5. what you might be doing at the store. _____

6. the first thing you are doing in the morning. _____

   7. what you are doing when you polish shoes. _____

   8. what you might be doing into the swimming pool.

   _____

   9. what you are doing if you are afraid you are late.

   _____

      10. what you are doing if you go to bed at midnight.

      _____ up late

      Which word means the opposite of *filling*? _____

      Which word starts to tell the reason why? _____

Write your Classroom Words from longest to shortest.

_____

_____

ALTERNATIVE HOMEWORK   Using five of your spelling words, write a
Time to Tell puzzle like the one above. Be sure to write the words you
use at the bottom of the page. Trade papers with another student and
work each other's puzzles.

In your reading book or textbooks find other words with *ing* added to a silent-*e* word. Send them to the moon by writing them on the spaceship before it blasts off!

Write the words you missed on the pretest.

_____

_____

_____

_____

Write the Outlaw Words and Classroom Words in color.

_____

_____

_____

_____

_____

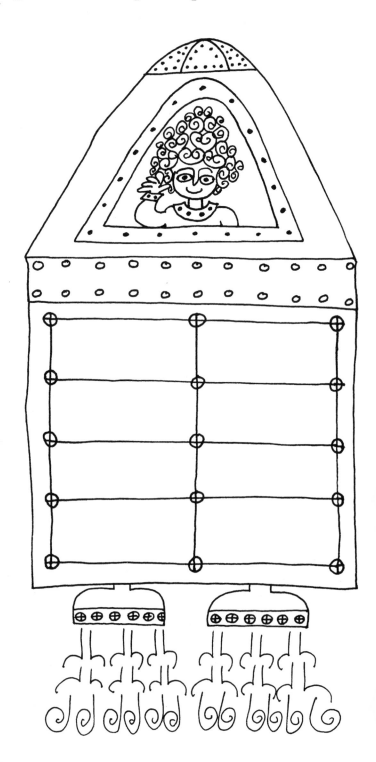

Be sure to study for your spelling test.

<u>ALTERNATIVE HOMEWORK</u>   Do the activity above.

Copy the words your teacher gives you under Classroom Words. Fold this page back along the dotted line so that only the Pretest column shows. Write the words your teacher dictates.

Spell*well* Words	Corrections	Pretest
1. chicken	_____	1. _____
2. desk	_____	2. _____
3. drank	_____	3. _____
4. hockey	_____	4. _____
5. neck	_____	5. _____
6. pink	_____	6. _____
7. pockets	_____	7. _____
8. snack	_____	8. _____
9. struck	_____	9. _____
10. unlock	_____	10. _____

Outlaw Words

11. who	_____	11. _____
12. whose	_____	12. _____
13. lose	_____	13. _____

Classroom Words

14. _____	_____	14. _____
15. _____	_____	15. _____
16. _____	_____	16. _____

Compare your words with the spelling list. Write the words you did not know in the Corrections column. If all, or all but one, of the words are correct, the following will be some of your spelling words: **necklace, checkers, jokingly, junkyard, silkworm,** and **unluckiest.** Write them in the Corrections column and do the Alternative Homework this week.

Sort your spelling words by their last letters and write them in the barrels. Then write other words that have the same ending next to the arrows.

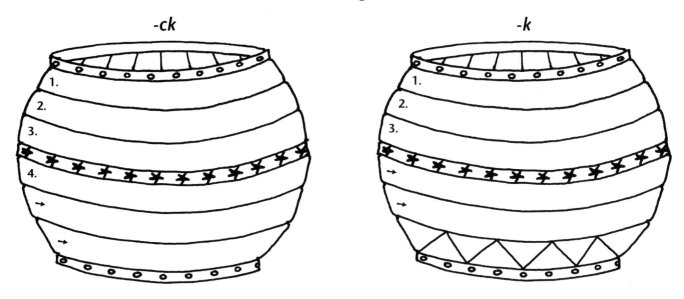

-ck

-k

Look at the words in the barrels. Circle the answers to the questions.

What kind of letter always comes before *ck*? (vowel or consonant?)

Does it have a long sound or a short sound?

What kind of letter comes before a single *k*? (vowel or consonant?)

Rule: Use *ck* at the _____ of a word (or syllable) after a _____ vowel.

Finish the words below with *k* or *ck*. Think about the rule you just learned.

1. pi_____   3. tan_____   5. mil_____

2. par_____   4. sa_____   6. tra_____

Write your Classroom Words, adding *s*, *ed*, or *er* if possible.

_____

_____

ALTERNATIVE HOMEWORK   In your reading book or textbooks find seven more words with *ck* or *k* that you want to learn. Write these words in the Corrections column on page 61. Then write the words and their definitions in your personal dictionary.

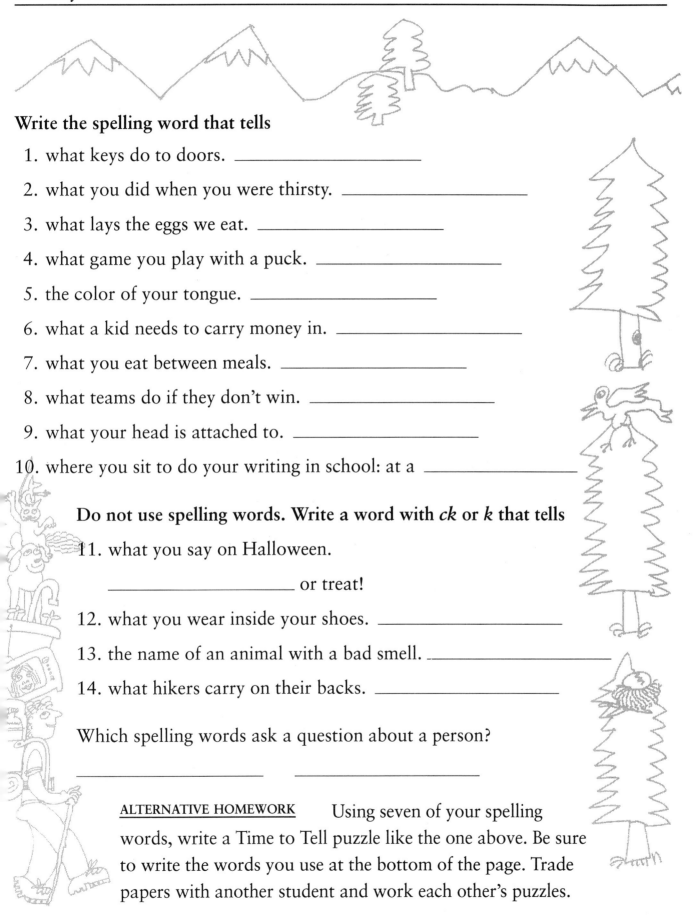

Write the spelling word that tells

1. what keys do to doors. _____

2. what you did when you were thirsty. _____

3. what lays the eggs we eat. _____

4. what game you play with a puck. _____

5. the color of your tongue. _____

6. what a kid needs to carry money in. _____

7. what you eat between meals. _____

8. what teams do if they don't win. _____

9. what your head is attached to. _____

10. where you sit to do your writing in school: at a _____

Do not use spelling words. Write a word with *ck* or *k* that tells

11. what you say on Halloween.

_____ or treat!

12. what you wear inside your shoes. _____

13. the name of an animal with a bad smell. _____

14. what hikers carry on their backs. _____

Which spelling words ask a question about a person?

_____ _____

ALTERNATIVE HOMEWORK   Using seven of your spelling words, write a Time to Tell puzzle like the one above. Be sure to write the words you use at the bottom of the page. Trade papers with another student and work each other's puzzles.

Write the spelling word that fits the category. Then write another word (not in the lesson) that also fits the category.

1. **Things with wings:** robin, plane, _____ , _____

2. **Sports:** football, tennis, _____ , _____

3. **Colors:** green, yellow, _____ , _____

4. **What you did to a glass of milk:** spilled, sipped, _____ ,

_____

5. **Parts of the body that bend:** knee, ankle, _____ , _____

6. **Things to do after school:** ride bikes, do homework, _____ ,

_____

7. **Things we do to a door:** push, shut, _____ , _____

8. **What you might do with a toy:** misplace, drop, _____ ,

_____

9. **Things made of wood:** pencil, chair, _____ , _____

10. **Places to carry things you need:** wallet, purse, _____ , _____

11. **What the batter did to the ball:** fouled, missed, _____ , _____

Write a spelling word that asks a question.

1. _____ dog is that?

2. _____ is your friend?

3. _____ is coming to the

party?

4. _____ is your favorite

movie star?

5. _____ house is the mail

truck stopping at?

ALTERNATIVE HOMEWORK   Do the activity above.

Find other *ck* words in your reading book or textbooks and send them to the moon by writing them on the spaceship before it blasts off!

Write the words you missed on the pretest.

_____

_____

_____

_____

Write your Classroom Words from longest to shortest.

_____

_____

_____

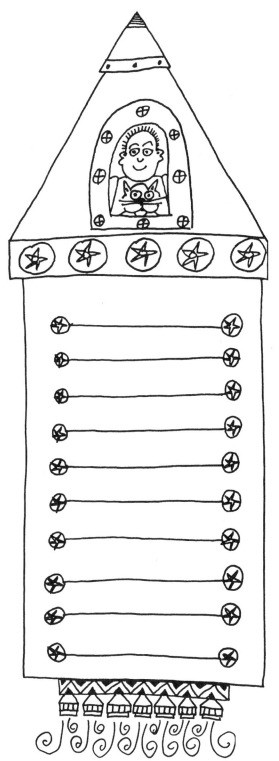

Be sure to study for your spelling test.

ALTERNATIVE HOMEWORK   Do the activity above.

PROGRESS CHART FOR WEEKLY SPELLING TESTS

Write the number of words you spelled correctly in the box under the lesson number.
Put a dot in the box next to that number.
Draw a line to connect the dots after each test.

NUMBER OF WORDS CORRECT	LESSON	1	2	3	4	5	6	7	8	9	10	11	12	13	14
	Ex. 16														
18															
17															
16	•														
15															
14															
13															
12															
11															
10															
9															
8															
7															
6															
5															
4															
3															
2															
1															
0															